GERMAN 20mm

IN WORLD WAR II

This emplaced 20mm quadruple flak is guarding an airfield in Russia.

1935 - 1945

Werner Müller

Schiffer Military/Aviation History
Atglen, PA

Sources

Engelmann-Scheibert, *Deutsche Artillerie 1934-1945* C.A. Starke Verlag

Koch, Horst-Adalbert, *Flak* Podzun-Pallas Verlag, Friedberg, 2nd Edition 1965

Müller, Werner, *Die leichte Flak 1906-1945*, Podzun-Pallas Verlage, Friedberg 1990

von Renz, Ott Wilhelm, *Deutsche Flugabwehr in 20. Jahrhundert*, Mittler Verlag 1973

Luftwaffe Service Manuals: L.Dv.400/Ia; L.Dv.400/Ib; L.Dv.400/Ic (draft); L.Dv.400Id; L.Dv.400/If; L.Dv.440 I; L.Dv.440/2; L.Dv.629; L.Dv.630 (draft); L.Dv.665/1; L.Dv.665/2; L.Dv.665/4; L.(Luft)1001; L.Dv.T.1003; L.Dv.T.1004; L.(Luft)T.1702

Navy Service Manual: M.Dv.Nr.576

Photo Credits

Bundesarchiv Koblenz; Military Technology Study Collection Koblenz; from the private archives of Wolfgang Fleischer, Dresden; Curt Galke, Oberhausen; Werner Müller, Bad Hersfeld; Dr. Hans-Dietrich Nicolaisen, Büsum; Erwin Niedringhaus, Oldenburg; Alfred Otte, Hannover; Professor Doctor Wolfgang Sawodny, Elchingen; Dr. Volker Seufert, Heidelberg; Elmar Widmann, Apfeltrach; as well as from some of the above-mentioned service manuals.

A 20mm flak in action in the winter of 1943-44 on the broad plains in Russia.

Translated from the German by David Johnston

Copyright © 1995 by Schiffer Publishing Ltd.

Printed in the United States of America.
ISBN: 0-88740-758-7

This title was originally published under the title,
Waffen-Arsenal Waffen und Fahrzeuge der Heere und Luftstreitkräfte 2 cm Flak im Einsatz 1935-1945,
by Podzun-Pallas-Verlag, Friedberg.

Published by Schiffer Publishing Ltd.
77 Lower Valley Road
Atglen, PA 19310
Please write for a free catalog.
This book may be purchased from the publisher.
Please include $2.95 postage.
Try your bookstore first.

We are interested in hearing from authors with book ideas on related topics.

20mm FLAK 28 OERLIKON

After World War One the Reichswehr was forbidden by Article 169 of the Versailles Treaty from having certain weapons, including anti-aircraft guns. After the Inter-Allied Military Control Commission withdrew in 1926, the practical training of motorized batteries to shoot at aerial targets was initiated, in secret of course, in the Reichswehr's motor transport battalions. The first light automatic weapon for engaging low-flying aircraft to reach the units, in 1928, was the Swiss-built 20mm Oerlikon. This weapon was purchased by many European states and during the Second World War they were captured by German troops in almost every theater. As the performance of the 20mm Flak 28 was comparable to that of the later German 20mm Flak 30 and 38, it was mainly used at home during the war. However because the shell casings were of a different shape than those of the German 20mm anti-aircraft guns, after the captured stocks of ammunition were used up a special facility had to be established to manufacture the casings, which were then fitted with the standard German 20mm projectile.

The Oerlikon was a recoil-operated weapon with mass locking and counterrecoil firing, which meant that when the trigger was pressed the breechblock shot forward under pressure from the counterrecoil spring. In counterrecoil the breechblock pushed the bottom shell from the 15-round magazine into the cartridge chamber. The firing pin was released just before the end of counterrecoil, striking the shell's ignition cap. The breech and the empty shell casing were stopped and finally forced back by the gases produced by the shot. The shell casing was ejected by the ejector during recoil. The weapon consisted of an air-cooled barrel, the casing, the breech assembly and the trigger housing with trigger. It was installed on a wheeled carriage, whose main components were cradle, upper carriage, lower carriage axle bearer with two wheels and three spars. With wheels attached, the carriage could be used as a split-trail carriage. With the wheels removed and a third spar installed it could be used as a tripod mount, or it could be installed on a pedestal mount. Two of the three spars were attached to the lower carriage in such a way that they formed the carriage trail when folded together. The third spar was inserted into the trail. Spreading the two spars which formed the gun trail, attaching the third on the opposite side, and removing the wheels resulted in a tripod mount.

The weapon was transportable when the wheels were attached to the lower carriage; it could travel with the muzzle facing to the front or rear. The normal mode of transport was the Kfz.81. For use in difficult terrain the weapon could be disassembled and moved by pack animal. With the axle bearer and carriage removed, the weapon could be placed on a special pedestal mount on a motor vehicle.

The sighting mechanism for use against aerial targets was initially a ring and bead sight. Both components of the gunsight were attached to a parallelogram which followed the cradle. Those Flak 28s which saw service in World War Two had as an aiming mechanism the Linealvisier 21 linear sight, consisting of a glass sight notch and a slide-mounted, revolving graduated circle which corresponded to range measurements. A crew of five, the gun commander and four gunners, was required to operate the 20mm Flak 28 with linear sight. The K1, or gun layer, aimed at the target and operated the trigger after the order to fire was given. The K2, or sight-gunner, set the ranges called out by the range-finder operator on the linear sight. The K3 observed the aerial target, estimated its direction of flight and any changes in altitude, and set these on the linear sight. The K4, or ammunition-gunner, loaded the magazine, monitored the ammunition feed, changed magazines and removed the empty shell casings.

With a muzzle velocity of 830 m/sec, the gun achieved a maximum firing range of 4,400 meters and a ceiling of 3,700 meters.

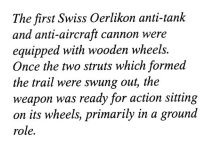

The first Swiss Oerlikon anti-tank and anti-aircraft cannon were equipped with wooden wheels. Once the two struts which formed the trail were swung out, the weapon was ready for action sitting on its wheels, primarily in a ground role.

Above:
The 20mm Flak 28 by Oerlikon in travelling position with its muzzle facing forward (in the direction of travel); the weapon could also be transported with the muzzle facing backward.

Above:
The wheels were removed for the tripod firing position. The two struts which formed the trail were swung out and the third strut was positioned to form the tripod.

At the time of the Polish Campaign in 1939, this 20mm Flak 28 Oerlikon was part of the anti-aircraft defenses of Döberitz-Elsgrund airfield, where Jagdgeschwader 1/132 "Richthofen" was based. The weapon's the 15-round magazine, which was installed from above, is clearly visible. In the semi-automatic fire mode the weapon was fired by means of a trigger lever on the right side of the trigger housing. On the left side there was a lever for full automatic fire, which could also be achieved by depressing the pedal-operated foot-trigger.

Left:
Another view of the 20mm Flak 28 in position at the airfield in Döberitz. The elevation handwheel is clearly visible on the upper mount, while to its left the horizontally-arranged handwheel for the traversing mechanism may just be seen.

20mm M.G.C/30L in S.L.30L

In 1931 the Reichswehr's first anti-aircraft units were equipped with two 20mm weapons, the Flak 28 and the M.G.C/30L in the S.L.30L pedestal mount, which was already in service with the navy. The weapon was recoil-operated with rocker arm locking. Its main components were: barrel with muzzle brake and barrel socket, cover and breech. The weapon was integrated with the motor mount, which incorporated the cocking mechanism and beneath which the 100-round T100-C/30 drum magazine was fitted. The motor mount flange was in turn attached to the pickup housing of the S.L.30L pedestal mount. Aiming was free-hand by means of a shoulder support and elevating grips, and the gunner had to adopt an uncomfortable squatting position at extreme angles of barrel elevation. When the gun was in a fixed pedestal mount, it was intended that a wooden grating should be installed around the gun, in order to allow better aiming at all elevations. Transportable versions of the weapon had the pedestal mounted on an outrigger-type gun mount, which was covered by a sheet-metal platform. Two sides of it were capable of being folded up while in travelling position on a twin-axle special trailer. Ammunition was fed from a drum magazine, which was installed empty on the motor mount. The drum then had to be filled with ammunition through the feed chute by means of a handcrank.

Although the ballistic values of the M.G.C/30L– with a firing range of approximately 4.8 kilometers, a ceiling of about 3,700 meters and a muzzle velocity of 900 m/sec–were not bad, the way the weapon was mounted and its lack of mobility proved less than Satisfactory

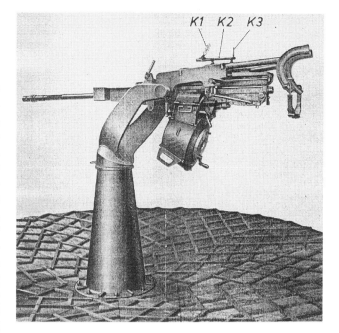

Above:
A 20mm Flak M.G.C./30 L installed in an S.L.30 L mount with drum magazine containing 98 rounds of ammunition. The folding auxiliary sight for aiming at aerial targets, which was mounted on a support (K2) above the pedestal mount, consisted of a front ring sight (K1) and a sight notch (K3). The individual sections of grating were put together around the pedestal mount.

Below Left:
As well as the pedestal mount, this aspect provides a good view of the MoL motor mount, in which the weapon was installed. It was of welded steel construction and was attached to the pedestal mount's pickup housing. The shoulder stock's twin yokes, which were covered with rubber pads, were mounted on two tubular spars extending back from the pickup housing.

Below:
The drum magazine with hand crank for filling same was attached to the motor mount from the left. Part of the continuous chain and the forward sprocket, both belonging to the cocking mechanism, may be seen above the mount housing.

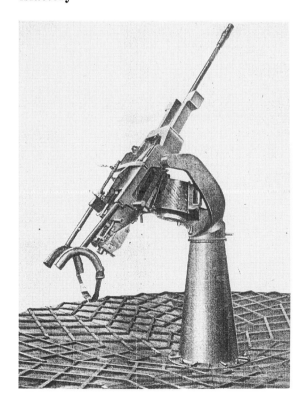

20mm FLAK 30 AND 38

By 1933 the M.G.C/30 had undergone significant modification, in particular in the area of the gun mount. The improved weapon was delivered to the field forces in 1934 as the 20mm Flak 30. Like its predecessor the weapon was recoil-operated; the barrel, gas cylinder plug and breech mechanism were locked together until after the projectile left the barrel. Loading, delivery of the next round and ejection of the empty casing were done through the pressure of the powder gas. The barrel was almost the same as that of the M.G.C/30L. However it was equipped with two types of muzzle brake. Well broken-in weapons used a muzzle with an interior diameter of 35 millimeters, while the 41mm muzzle, which had less of a recoil braking effect, was used on new weapons, in difficult operating conditions of cold or rain, or with specially-marked ammunition.

Ammunition was fed into the Flak 30 from a flat magazine, which held twenty rounds, mounted on the left side.

The gun carriage consisted of stationary triangular bottom mount with a bracket for attaching to the single-axle Sonderanhänger 51 trailer. Mounted on the bottom gun carriage was the revolving upper gun carriage with the cradle, which was capable of movement in the vertical plane. The elevating mechanism was arranged on the right side of the upper gun carriage, and behind it was the traversing mechanism, where the gunner's seat was also attached. The weapon was held by a sleigh mount which slid on rails.

Installed in the cradle was the braking cylinder, which limited the sleigh mount's recoil when the gun was fired and controlled its counterrecoil through fluid braking. The trigger mechanism was operated by the gun layer (K1) by means of a foot pedal on the right for semi-automatic fire and one on the left for full-automatic fire. He used either the Flakvisier 35 or the Linealvisier 21 gunsights for engaging aerial targets, and the 3 x 8 degrees telescopic sight for ground targets.

The improved Flak 38 reached the field forces in 1939; however, its ballistic values were the same as those of the 20mm Flak 30, because it used the same ammunition. Nevertheless the theoretical rate of fire was increased from the 280-300 rounds per minute of the Flak 30 to 480 rounds per minute, while the practical rate of fire was raised from 120 to 220 rounds per minute. Rates of traverse and elevation were improved through the addition of an overdrive to each mechanism. One turn of the elevation handwheel raised the barrel 4 degrees, 12 degrees in overdrive; the traverse handwheel turned the gun 10 degrees per turn and 30 degrees in overdrive. The gun layer no longer sat behind the weapon, but beside it on the right. He operated the horizontal handwheel of the traversing mechanism with his left hand and the vertically-mounted elevation handwheel, which was located on the right side of the gun mount, with his right.

Below: A 20mm Flak 30 in an emplacement on the North Sea coast of Belgium, 1940-41.

A recoil mechanism was built into the interior of the cradle box. It absorbed the weapon's recoil and returned the sleigh mount to the forward position after firing. What had been achieved by the braking cylinder of the Flak 30 was now accomplished by a spring assembly in conjunction with the muzzle brake. With only minor modifications this recoil mechanism could also be installed in the 20mm Flak 30. The trigger mechanism was activated by the gun layer by means of a foot pedal. A lever on the right side of the breech allowed him to select semi-automatic or full-automatic fire and engage or disengage the safety.

A noticeable external change on the Flak 38 compared to the Flak 30 were the two bearing rings with bearing caps bolted on to the cradle. The right bearing ring housed the gear segment for the elevating mechanism and two adjustable elevating stops.

Two gunsights were available; the Flakvisier 38 was used for engaging aerial targets and the 3x8 degrees telescopic against ground targets.

The 20mm Flak 30 and 38 went into action on the Sonderanhänger 51 trailer or mounted on trucks, self-propelled carriages, tracked vehicles, and railway cars. They were also used on fixed pedestal mounts.

With a muzzle velocity of 900 meters per second, the Flak 38 achieved a maximum firing range of 4,800 meters and a ceiling of 3,800 meters.

Above: A 20mm Flak 30 on a high platform in Norway.

Right:
Today this 20mm Flak sits in the Rudel Barracks in Rendsburg.

Below:
The 20mm Flak 38 gun carriage with Flakvisier 38 anti-aircraft gun sight. Noticeable are the two bearing rings, which were not present on the Flak 30 carriage.

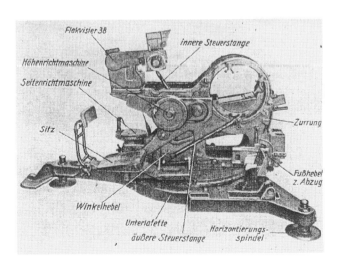

The crew of a 20mm Flak 30 wearing full equipment beside their gun shortly before the outbreak of war. The men are still equipped with an obsolete type of gas mask. The range-finder operator sitting on the right is wearing the shoulder-mount for the R 36 range-finder but has not yet placed the range-finder in operating position. The shoulder-mount alone weighed 5 kilograms.

Men of a Germany-based flak battery practice with their 20mm guns. They were employed to protect the Leitz Firm in Wetzlar. (Taken on August 2, 1942)

A 20mm Flak emplacement on the North African coast.

A 20mm Flak guards a military bridge over the Nieman (Memel) near Prienau in 1941.

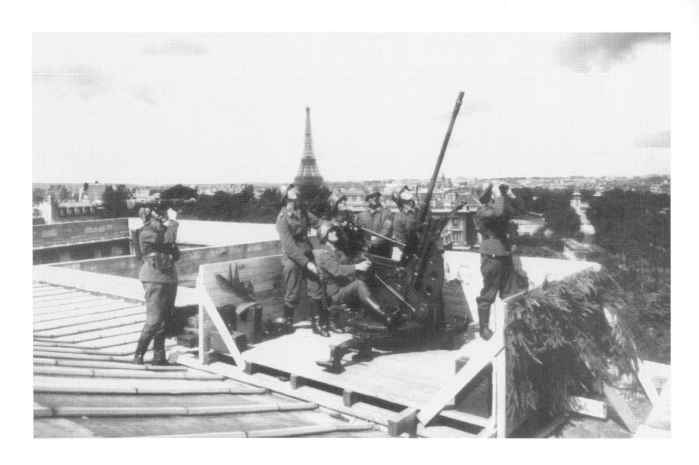

A 20mm Flak on guard above the rooftops of Paris.

This 20mm flak post was located on the Daniel 6, a ship that formed one of the supports of the "Mudra Bridge."

A 20mm Flak 30 in position above the bridge over the Volga River at Rzhev, 1942.

20mm Flak 38s stand ready to repel an enemy attack, together with a battery of 88mm anti-aircraft guns, seen in the background.

Left:
A downright airy 20mm flak platform in Norway. One bomb exploding nearby would have been enough to bring down the structure and crew together with their gun.

Below:
Even while eating from his mess tin, the gunner sat in his seat behind the 20mm flak, ready to defend against a sudden attack by low-flying enemy aircraft on the military bridge in the river valley below.

In order to release soldiers for service at the front, beginning in 1942 members of the Hitler Youth were used as anti-aircraft artillery auxiliaries in home-based flak batteries. The blue-grey uniform they wore resembled that of the Luftwaffe. It consisted of a tunic with patch pockets, with the Luftwaffe emblem sewed on above the right one, long pants, a leather belt with the Luftwaffe belt buckle, and a ski cap or in action a steel helmet. The arm band of the Hitler Youth had to be worn on the left, upper sleeve of the tunic. Both photographs show an anti-aircraft artillery auxiliary crew with a 20mm Flak 30 during service of the piece drills. The gun emplacement is surrounded by wooden boxes filled with earth, protection for the crew against shrapnel.

The most difficult way of moving a 20mm Flak in terrain was surely by hand.

A more comfortable, though slower and rather unmilitary mode of transporting the gun was by ox team, as here during a change of positions in the Balkans.

Rest stop for a flak battery of the "Hermann Göring" Division. The guns are mounted on medium personnel carriers with supporting axles. The trailers carry ammunition and the personal effects of the gun crew.

20mm Flak crossing a military bridge. It is being towed by a light Krupp L2H 143 truck.

This 20mm Flak has been loaded on to a 3-ton Ford Maultier V8. Once again a trailer is used to haul baggage and ammunition.

A Ford Maultier with 20mm Flak 38 drives out of the blast pen where the vehicle and its mounted gun had been parked.

This 20mm Flak 38 is mounted on a camouflaged light prime mover, the Sd.Kfz. 10/4. The white collar tabs on the uniforms of the gun crew identify them as members of the "Hermann Göring" Division.

Here we see the Sd.Kfz. 10/4 light prime mover with a 20mm Flak 38. Boxes of ammunition are lined up on the sideboards, which have been folded down into the horizontal position. These served to enlarge the platform when the gun was in action. The boxes over the front fenders contain the gun crew's rifles (Karabiner 98k).

Left:
The radiator and driver's compartment of this light self-propelled carriage have been lightly armored. Judging by the symbols on the gun shield of the mounted 20mm flak, the gun's crew were extremely successful with their weapon.

Below:
These 20mm Flak mounted on light self-propelled carriages sit well-camouflaged in a jumping-off position. The loading ramps in front of the radiator of the vehicle in the foreground are noteworthy. These were attached to the gun platform's folded-down rear panel. With the help of two cables attacked to the Sonderanhänger 51 trailer, which ran over pulleys located on the left and right sides of the vehicle behind the front seat, two men pulled the gun onto the self-propelled carriage. Here the left-hand pulley is visible above the steering wheel. After the gun had been lowered onto the bed of the vehicle, the trailer was rolled back down the ramps again.

Here a 20mm Flak 38 is mounted on an armored troop carrier (Sd.Kfz. 251/17) of the "Hermann Göring" Division (note division emblem). The side panels could be folded down. The rifles were stowed in the box beside the driver's compartment.

A battery of 20mm Quadruple Flak on the march. The guns are mounted on lightly-armored, camouflaged 4.5-ton trucks. Sonderanhänger 36 trailers contained the crew's equipment as well as ammunition for the guns.

Above:

In 1942 the 20mm Flak 38 was mounted on the chassis of the 38 (t) medium tank, Sd.Kfz. 140. Although the result was an armored, fully tracked vehicle for the flak, it proved unsatisfactory on account of the small 20mm gun. Another disadvantage was the need to fold down the upper armored side panels when engaging surface targets. This reduced even further the protection offered the crew by the open-topped fighting compartment. The weapon was mounted on the rear of the vehicle, as the engine was located in the middle.

Left:

A frontal view of the vehicle; note the driver's open vision port. In the fighting compartment one can see the barrel of the 20mm Flak 38, the deflector bag and above it the pivoted ring sight.

The three photographs on this page were taken in the Military Technology Study Collection in Koblenz. Above left is a 20mm Flak-Zwilling 38 in the M 44 double mount. Above right is a rare Flak-Zwilling 38 in a double mount, transportable on a single-axle Sonderanhänger 51 trailer.

Below right:
This 20mm Flak-Drilling 151 was created by mounting three MG 151/20 aircraft cannon in the Fla S1 151 pedestal-type anti-aircraft gun mount.

MG 151/20 IN THREE-BARREL MOUNT

By late in the war production of the 20mm Flak 38 was no longer able to keep up with demand. Consequently other weapons, including 20mm aircraft cannon, were employed as anti-aircraft guns, most often in three-barrel mounts which lacked elevating or traversing mechanisms and which thus had to be aimed freehand. The number of enemy aircraft shot down by them was low because of the absence of these mechanisms, however their high rate of fire and the resulting volume of tracer allowed them to be effective in defending a target against direct low-level attack.

The guns were capable of being rotated through 360 degrees, but elevation was limited to -3 degrees to +49 degrees with the help of a horizontal tube attached to the cradle, at the end of which were grips. These were linked to the trigger mechanism. The left grip fired the middle weapon, while the right one fired the two outside weapons. The MG 151/20 was used on motor torpedo boats, in the home defense, to protect factories, on railroad trains and on armored troop carriers.

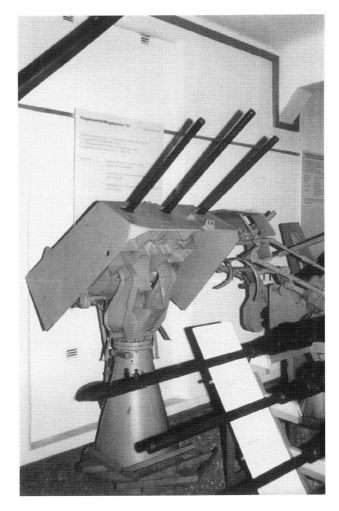

Left:
Anti-aircraft MG 151/20s in the 151 D triple-mount, seen here installed on an Sd.Kfz. 251/21 armored troop carrier. Each of the three cannon had a theoretical rate of fire of 720 rounds per minute, which naturally made freehand aiming very difficult. The oblique muzzles on the two outer weapons are noteworthy. Their purpose was to reduce the moment of rotation on the mount caused by the recoil of the outer guns

Below:
An Sd.Kfz. 251/21 armored troop carrier with the anti-aircraft MG 151/ 20 cannon in a triple mount.

20mm FLAKVIERLING 38

In 1940 the flak arm picked up on an idea of the navy's, to place four 20mm anti-aircraft guns in a carriage on a triangular base. The weapon would be transportable on a Sonderanhänger 52 single-axle trailer. The four-barrelled flak was either installed on a receiving pedestal on railway cars to guard transport trains, or in a receiving ring equipped with levellers on self-propelled carriages – prime movers and half-tracked vehicles – and the chassis of the Panzer IV as the "Wirbelwind" (Whirlwind) and "Möbelwagen" (Furniture Van) anti-aircraft tanks.

The ballistic data of the 20mm Flakvierling were the same as those of the 20mm Flak 38. However the range of elevation extended from -10 degrees to +100 degrees, beyond the vertical. The weapon was feared by the enemy on account of its great firepower. In theory it could fire 1,800 rounds per minute, but its practical rate of fire was 800 rounds per minute on account of the requirement to change magazines. Enemy aircraft found themselves in a veritable curtain of shellfire, one made visible through the use of tracing ammunition.

The 20mm Flakvierling 38 carriage consisted of the triangular base with the attached racer. Mounted in bearings on the racer was the 360 degrees rotatable upper carriage. This in turn supported the cradle, which moved in the vertical plane. Mounted on both was the trigger mechanism, which was activated by the gun layer (K1) by means of two foot pedals. Each foot pedal moved the trigger guards of two diagonally-opposed guns. In this way it was possible to maintain full-automatic fire. While two weapons fired the magazines of the other two were replaced. Pressing both foot pedals fired all four weapons. The gun layer's adjustable seat was positioned behind the upper carriage. The elevation and traverse mecha-nisms with the traversing drive as well as the sight mount were positioned in front of it. The platforms with magazine storage were bolted under the upper carriage on the left and right. The compensator and the spent-shell-casing collector box were at the front of the upper carriage. Two sliding sleigh mounts were arranged on each of the cradle caps. These carried the 20mm Flak 38 weapons and were connected to the recoil mechanism by lugs.

Several types of gunsight were used; the Flakvisier 40, the Linealvisier 21 or the Schwebe-kreisvisier 30/38 (pivoted ring sight) for engaging aerial targets, and the 3 x 8 degrees telescopic sight for ground targets.

The carriage was equipped with a gun shield for use in the ground role.

Above right:
This 20mm Flak 38 is in the Military Technology Study Collection in Koblenz.

Right:
20mm Flak 38 seen from the right front.

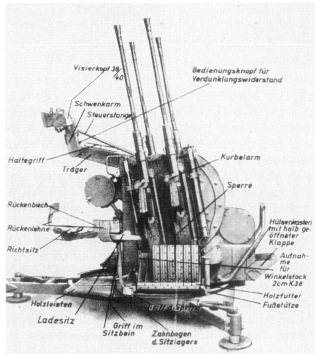

Visierkopf 38/40
Bedienungsknopf für Verdunklungswiderstand
Schwenkarm
Steuerstange
Haltegriff
Träger
Kurbelarm
Sperre
Rückenblech
Rückenlehne
Richtsitz
Hülsenkasten mit halb geöffneter Klappe
Aufnahme für Winkelstock 2cm K.38
Holzleisten
Griff d. Sperre
Holzfutter Fußstütze
Ladesitz
Griff im Sitzbein
Zahnbogen d. Sitzlagers

This view of the 20mm Flakvierling 38 provides an excellent view of the deflector box, in which spent shell casings collected, in front, and the magazine rack on the right. (Military Technology Study Collection, Koblenz)

20mm Flakvierling 38, seen from the right with barrels elevated to approximately 100 degrees.

This 20mm Flakvierling was placed aboard a ferry to defend a water-based barrage balloon unit. The gun crew are wearing life jackets.

20mm Flakvierling 38 on a Sonderanhänger 52 trailer.

The crew of a 20mm Vierlingsflak manhandles its gun into position.

Left:
The 20mm Flakvierling 38 was used in every theater of the war on account of its great firepower. Here the crew of the Number Two gun of Lei-Hei. 30/XI stands ready to fire at the Hindenburg Lock in Anderten near Hannover. One member of the crew had to be in the gunner's seat at all times.

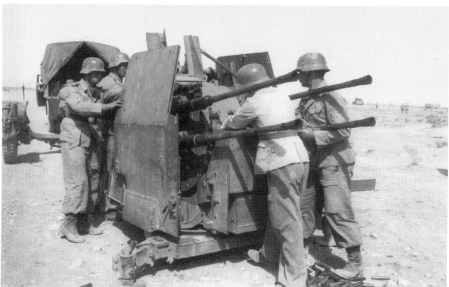

Center left:
A 20mm Flakvierling is prepared for a move to a new position on the broad North African plain. The gun has yet to be loaded aboard its trailer; however, the side panels of the armor shield have already been folded back into the travelling position. The Sonderanhänger 51 trailer waits to receive the gun. In front of the emptied casing box lie the spent shell casings.

Below:
A 20mm Flakvierling in Africa firing against a ground target. A cloud of dust was stirred up as soon as the gun commenced firing, making subsequent accurate aiming difficult.

Winter action in Russia. The 20mm Vierling was painted white for better camouflage and the crew are wearing white winter clothing.

Each foot pedal fired two diagonally-opposed weapons. Meanwhile the magazines feeding the other two weapons could be changed without calling for a cessation of fire. Depressing both foot pedals fired all four guns, which is apparently the case here. Boxes containing reserve ammunition have been arrayed around the gun emplacement.

Flak protection on the concrete wall of the Eckertal Dam in the Harz Mountains, winter 1943-44. The anti-aircraft defenses of important dams were beefed up following the British attacks on the Eder Dam in May 1943.

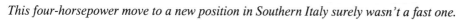

This four-horsepower move to a new position in Southern Italy surely wasn't a fast one.

The crew of a 20mm Vierling on a self-propelled carriage tracks an incoming target. The gun commander waits for the range-finder operator with his one-meter R36 range-finder to call out the optimum range for engaging the target before giving the order to open fire.

A battery of 20mm Flakvierlinge on self-propelled carriages at readiness in a wood.

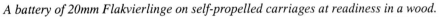

Above:
Two 20mm Flakvierlinge on self-propelled carriages ready to fire while guarding a main road in Northern Russia, winter 1943-44.

Left:
As the photos on this page illustrate, the 20mm Flakvierling on a self-propelled carriage offered a good target on account of its great muzzle height. As digging into the hard, frozen ground was impossible, the crews had to hope that the gun's camouflage finish, their white winter clothing and any additional camouflage that they could find for gun and vehicle would be enough to prevent them from being spotted too soon.

20mm FLAK ON RAILWAY AND ARMORED TRAINS

Beginning in 1941, two types of railway flak battalion were formed: Heavy Railway Flak Battalions, which acted as mobile reserves which could be moved to wherever they were needed by the German air defense, and Light Railway Flak Battalions, which were to guard transport trains from air attack. The year 1942 saw the introduction of Light Rail Transport Protection Flak Battalions.

For railway train defense 20mm Flak 30, Flak 38 or Flakvierling 38 weapons were placed on twin-axle open flatcars with side-racks. The guns could be set up either on their triangular bases or on fixed mounts. By removing the side-rails and installing special superstructures and fittings, the Reichsbahn (German State Railway) converted standard freight cars into light flak cars: the Gun Car I (E) Light Flak and the Gun Car II (E) Light Flak. Both types of car included living quarters as well as a gun platform. As may be seen in the sketch below, the modifications included crew living quarters, toilet facility, storage shelves, the gun platform, barrel deflectors to protect the locomotive and other cars from being hit, and the splinterproof walls. Only the Gun Car I had the latter. They surrounded the gun platform to a height of about 1.1 meters. The space between the inner and outer walls was filled with slightly-reinforced concrete. The side-walls of the Gun Car II's gun platform, which sat about 1.1 meters above the floor of the car, could be folded down into a horizontal position to give the gun crew more room to move about when in action.

We have provided only a few sample photos of 20mm anti-aircraft guns on armored trains in this volume, and we refer the reader to the commercially-available literature on the subject.

Above:
A view of Light Flak Gun Car I (E), armed with a 20mm Flak 38. The gun mount was bolted to the wooden platform of the gun car. Clearly visible is the barrel deflector frame, which prevented the gun from hitting the cars in front with its fire. To the right and left of the entrance to the crew living quarters are shelves for storing accessories and a quantity of ammunition. The double-walled sides protected the crew from fragments. The space between the walls was filled with iron-reinforced concrete. The ladder lying on the roof of the living quarters was leaned against the side of the car for the crew to climb down. It was planned to install wooden steps inside the car for this purpose.

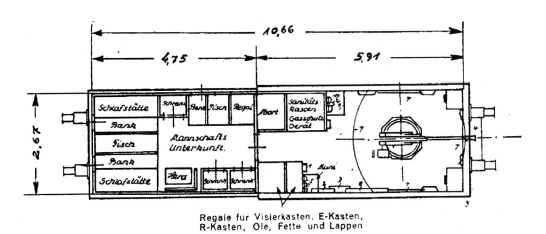

Regale fur Visierkasten. E-Kasten,
R-Kasten, Ole, Fette und Lappen

1. Gewehrständer
2. Schanzzeug
3. Entlader
4. Rohrkasten
5. Stahlhelme
6. Geschützüberzug
7. Abweisbügel

Left:
This sketch shows the layout of the rooms and the arrangement of equipment on the Light Flak Gun Car I (E).

The Light Flak Gun Car II (E) with a 20mm Flakvierling 38 in firing position. (1) Crew accommodations, consisting of beds for eight men, tables, benches, two small closets with another built into the storage area, and a stove, whose stovepipe (31) had to be folded down when the gun was in firing position; (2) ladder for access to the quarters; (30) hand brake; (28) the storage area beneath the gun platform was accessible by way of three doors in the front and side walls or directly from the crew living quarters; (5) struts, which braced the folded-down sides against the storage space; (6) a hinge-mounted railing.

Left:
A view of the gun platform of the Gun Car II (E) armed with a Flak 38. This sat 1.1 meters above the floor of the car and could be reached from the crew quarters by means of a set of steps. The gun and its triangular base sat on a wooden base pedestal (11); (10) wooden boxes, each of which held ten boxes of magazines for 20mm flak ammunition; (8 and 9) bolts and metal bands for releasing the folding side walls.

Two flak cars such as this one accompanied special trains belonging to Hitler, Göring and other functionaries. Mussolini received two of these special flak cars from Hitler as a gift. There was a 20mm Flakvierling emplacement at each end of the car. Between the gun positions were the quarters for the car's 17-man crew, which was provided by the General Göring Regiment, as well as storage areas for ammunition, equipment and baggage.

This interim flak car was part of Armored Train No. 26 in 1942. While the train was under way the side panels of the gun's armor shield were folded back to reduce air resistance. Curiously, there is no barrel deflector discernable in the direction of the crew quarters.

Left:
With the increased threat of fighter-bomber attack, flak cars were added to passenger and service trains. Here a 20mm Flakvierling on a high-speed train entering the main station in Brussels.

Right:
This 20mm Flakvierling was deployed on Armored Train No. 28, a former Russian train that was converted to normal European gauge and also underwent other modifications.

Left:
This photo shows an 88mm flak battery mounted on standard freight cars, a local improvisation, near Rzhev in January 1942. Providing anti-aircraft protection are two 20mm Gebirgsflak 38 on the freight car in the foreground. These weapons had a fixed gun shield and a gun mount of stamped metal construction and tripod configuration. The gun weighed only 276 kilograms in firing position, compared to the 420 kilograms of the Flak 38.
Ballistics and ammunition were the same as the Flak 38. These guns are equipped with the Linealvisier 21 linear sight. The empty shell casings in the snow are an indication that the guns have recently seen action.

The gun and flak car of the standard Type BP42 armored train was armed with a 76.2mm F.F.295/1(r) cannon and a 20mm four-barrelled Vierlingsflak 38 on a raised stand. Both photos show the gun and flak car of Armored Train 63, whose emblem was the rising sun. The hinges for the folding sections of the parapet on the flak platform are noteworthy. Visible beneath them are the closed flaps over vision slots and rifle and machine-gun ports. The 20mm platform was connected to the following car by a crawlway.

Left:
A 20mm Flakvierling 38 on Armored Train 51. While the train was on the move the muzzles were protected by muzzle covers and the side panels of the gun shield were folded back.

This 20mm Flak 38 with gun shield was placed on a lightly-armored flak car as part of Armored Train 22, a captured Polish train which was modified and returned to service by the Germans. Behind it is the revolving turret and 75mm cannon of the forward gun position. This photo shows the train in action in France in 1941.

Camouflaged flak position with 20mm four-barrelled flak on Armored Train 72A.

A 20mm Flak 38 with gun shield on the gun car of Armored Train No. 1 (1941-42). Visible behind the 20mm flak is a Böhler-Type 47mm Infantry Cannon. Note that the gun car has armored sides.

20mm FLAKVIERLING ON FLAK TOWERS

During the course of the war, flak towers were built to guard the downtown areas of Berlin, Hamburg and Vienna. As a rule these gun towers contained four 128mm double-barrel anti-aircraft guns. Mounted on special side-platforms were 37mm or 20mm Flakvierling anti-aircraft guns, whose responsibility it was to repel attacks by low-flying aircraft on the gun or fire-control towers. The lower portions of several of these flak towers included shelters for the civilian population. Quarters for personnel manning the equipment and guns were located beneath the concrete roof. Ammunition was delivered to the guns by special elevators.

Left:
While the flak tower in Heiligengeist Field in Hamburg was still under construction, four-barrelled anti-aircraft guns were placed on several of the still-uncompleted platforms to protect the construction site.

Below:
A view of one of the corner platforms for light flak on the master tower at Heiligengeist Field in Hamburg with a 20mm four-barrelled flak. The crew is engaged in service of the piece drills. Standing off to the side is the range-finder operator with his 1-meter R 36 range-finder. He is wearing the device in the operating position on the shoulder mount.

Above:
One of the 20mm four-barrelled anti-aircraft guns on the gun tower in Berlin Friedrichshain. In the left background may be seen the tower of city hall.

Right:
The Number Three gun of 2/1.414 with its crew on the Heiligengeist Field flak tower in Hamburg.

FLAK BATTLE FERRIES AND FLAK TRANSPORT FERRIES

Several Ferry Flak Battalions were created as special units in early 1942. They were employed on Lake Ladoga as part of the German encirclement of Leningrad, in the waters off the Crimean Peninsula, between Sicily and North Africa and on the Danube during the Battle of Budapest.

The Flak Battle Ferries consisted of a platform mounted on two large seaworthy, shallow-draft pontoons, on which four 88mm Flak 18 or 36 guns, two 20mm Flak 30 or 38 light anti-aircraft guns and a 4-meter R(H) range-finder with command computer were mounted with cleats and bolts. In tactical terms, these ferries were strictly anti-aircraft vehicles. The overall weight of four 88mm guns with crew and ammunition plus two 20mm guns with crew and ammunition plus four-meter range-finder with computer and crew as well as the radio equipment with mast, antenna and operators, was barely 50 tons.

As their name would suggest, the role of flak transport ferries was to provide anti-aircraft protection for the transport of goods or troops. The total weight of the ferry's load and defensive weapons could not exceed 50 tons. Different armament combinations were used depending on the mission, whether it be defense against attacks from land, sea or air. The possible combinations were too numerous to be related here. The most commonly used weapons on the main and secondary platforms were the 20mm Flak 30 and 38, the 37mm Flak 36 and one or two 88mm Flak 18 or 36.

The secondary platforms were removable and could be located all about the ferry. These ferries were often referred to as "Siebel Ferries" after their designer, Reserve Oberstleutnant Siebel, or "SS Ferries" (SS = sehr schwere, or very heavy).

Above:
Two 20mm Flak 30 anti-aircraft guns have been placed on the main platform of this flak-transport ferry, also called a "Siebel Ferry" in honor of its designer. This was one way of arming the ferry's main platform. The guns were secured to the deck by means of a clamp on each levelling disc. The angled part of the clamp fitted over the edge of the levelling disc, while the opposite end lodged in a support plate which was screwed to the ferry's floorboards.

Left:
Mounted on the main platform of this flak-transport ferry is a 37mm Flak 38, while the two secondary platforms each house a 20mm Flak 30.

An 88mm Flak 18 was mounted in the center of the stern of this flak-transport ferry while two 20mm Flak 30 were installed on the main platform.

Right:
A 20mm Flak 30, mounted on the secondary platform on the port side of a flak-transport ferry. (1) Box containing replacement barrels; (2) magazine boxes; (3) airtight ammunition boxes; (4) box containing illuminating apparatus; (5) box containing the rangefinder; (6) ammunition pouches as well as additional boxes of 20mm ammunition for the Flak 30 and machine-gun ammunition; (7) flak gunsight box.

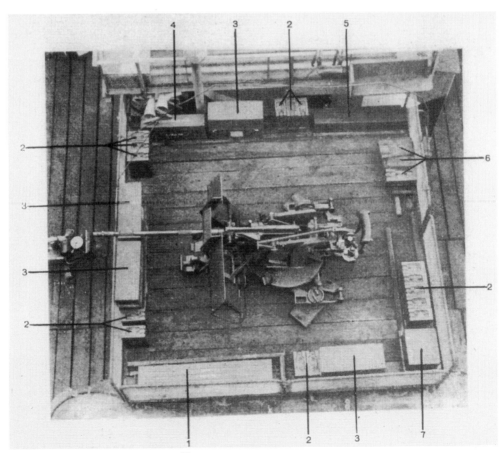

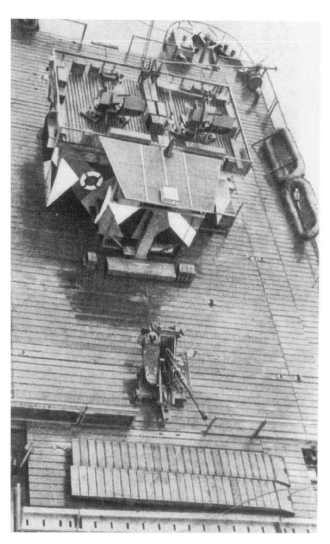

Above:
20mm anti-aircraft gun on a flak ferry in the Strait of Kerch.

Above:
A 37mm Flak 36 on the bow of a flak-transport ferry, with two 20mm Flak 30 with gun shield on the main platform.

Below:
A "Siebel Ferry" on a training voyage. Accurate defensive fire from such a ferry was possible only on very calm water, since the guns lacked the levelling devices which compensated for the rolling motion of the ship which were standard equipment on the navy's guns.

20mm FLAK IN SERVICE WITH THE NAVY
20mm FLAK 29 AND 20mm FLAK 29 APT. IN 20mm PEDESTAL MOUNT 40

The 20mm Flak 29 and the Flak 29 apt. in the Sockellafette 40 pedestal mount were intended by the navy for installation on ships, primarily to engage air and sea targets. They were therefore movable about three axes. Two of these served to move the weapon in azimuth and elevation, while the third enabled the weapon to be levelled when the ship was pitching and rolling.

This automatic weapon was built according to the Oerlikon mass locking system, and space limitations prevent us from providing a more detailed description here. The differences between the two weapons were minor, the most obvious outward difference being the Flak 29 apt.'s lack of a cone-shaped flash suppressor.

The weapons were aimed with the aid of two grips which projected to the sides and a shoulder stirrup. A belt which went around his back held the gunner firmly in the shoulder stirrup. The sighting mechanism consisted of a ring sight with fork-shaped aiming notch. The extent of traverse was unlimited through 360 degrees. The range of elevation was from -8 degrees to +100 degrees. The range of movement of the levellers was 15 degrees to both sides.

Full-automatic fire was produced by twisting the left handgrip. Semi-automatic fire was possible by means of a lever on the weapon. Shells were fed from a drum magazine containing 60 rounds, which was mounted on the upper, left side of the gun. Empty shell casings were ejected to the right into a bag. The weapon was unable to achieve its theoretical rate of fire of 500-600 rounds per minute on account of the need to change the magazine after firing sixty rounds. Maximum firing range was about 4,400 meters, ceiling about 2,700 meters.

In order to spare the gunner an uncomfortable squatting position at high barrel elevations, the gun and cradle could be raised or lowered by a member of the gun crew with the help of a handwheel on the cylindrical lower mount.

Above:
The 20mm 29 apt in the 20mm Pedestal Mount 40, seen here in the anti-aircraft position. The weapon could be raised or lowered by using the large handwheel on the mount, in order to ease freehand aiming and tracking of moving targets by the gunner.

Right:
The gun seen from the right, with shoulder stirrups, folding ring sight and fork-shaped sighting notch, deflector bag for spent shell casings and handwheel for raising or lowering the column and gun. This handwheel could be rotated around the mount, so that the man operating the wheel could follow the gunner.

Both photos show the 20mm Oerlikon MK I on the MK II AA mount with adjustable-height gun mount in service with the navy. Above the gun is installed on a navy vessel, below in an emplacement ashore. The size of the large drum magazine is noteworthy.

The 20mm Flakvierling C38 was also used on larger navy vessels. The naval version of the four-barrelled flak differed from that of the army in that it required an azimuth and an elevation setter, both sitting in front of the gun, and an angle setter. The latter compensated for the pitching and rolling movements of the ship by means of a large handwheel (lower photo).

Above:
The gun crew at battle stations beside their 20mm four-barrelled flak; all are wearing life jackets. The large handwheel for adjusting the angle of the gun is a prominent feature.

Left:
Visible on the front of the gun are the two unoccupied seats for the traverse and elevation setters and their uncovered aiming mechanisms, which were connected. Two members of the crew scan the sky. One wears a telephone set, consisting of a throat microphone and a headset, with which he could contact the fire-direction center.

46

FLAKPANZER (ANTI-AIRCRAFT TANKS) WITH 20mm FLAK

The following photographs of 20mm Flakvierling on the chassis of the Panzer IV will be familiar to the experts. Unfortunately the author has been unable to uncover any new photographs of the "Möbelwagen" or "Wirbelwind" anti-aircraft tanks. Perhaps some of our readers can help with new photos.

The "Möbelwagen" (photo below) was not a true tank, because the fighting compartment for the 20mm Flakvierling was open on top. In fact, in battle the vertical armor plates had to be lowered to the horizontal position, where they offered the crew no protection whatever. The combat weight of the "Möbelwagen" was 25 tons. Its armor was 10 to 80 millimeters thick. With its 272 H.P. motor the vehicle achieved a top speed of 38 kph. The crew consisted of the tank commander, a gunner, two loaders and the driver.

Closer to a true anti-aircraft tank was the "Wirbelwind", with the 20mm Flakvierling 38 enclosed in a revolving turret on a Panzer IV chassis. True, the turret was still open on top, for ventilation and to provide an unrestricted field of view on account of the lack of radar, but a clever arrangement of the armor plates left enough room for the commander, a gunner and two loaders during combat. The vehicle's performance was the same as that of the "Möbelwagen", namely 272 H.P. and 38 kph. At 22 tons, combat weight was slightly less than the "Möbelwagen", although armor protection was the same 16-80 millimeters.

On account of its appearance with its armor panels raised, this anti-aircraft tank, a 20mm four-barrelled flak on the chassis of a Panzer IV, was dubbed the Möbelwagen (furniture van). Here the side panels are at an angle of about 30 degrees for engaging aerial targets. They were held in this position by hinged plates installed in the front and rear.

The Spielberger German Armor & Military Vehicles Series

Panther & Its Variants
WALTER J. SPIELBERGER

Size: 8 1/2" x 11" 288 pages hard cover
over 460 photographs
ISBN: 0-88740-397-2 $39.95

Sturmgeschütz & Its Variants
WALTER J. SPIELBERGER

Size: 8 1/2" x 11" 256 pages hard cover
over 240 photographs
ISBN: 0-88740-398-0 $39.95

Panzer III & Its Variants
WALTER J. SPIELBERGER

Size: 8 1/2" x 11" 168 pages hard cover
over 200 photographs
ISBN: 0-88740-448-0 $29.95

Panzer IV & Its Variants
WALTER J. SPIELBERGER

Size: 8 1/2" x 11" 168 pages hard cover
over 200 photographs
ISBN: 0-88740-515-0 $29.95